MW01241545

WILDERNESS ENCOUNTER

A STEPPING STONE TO SELF- AWARENESS

AND SELF- RESPECT

SUSAN BRIGGS OSBORN

WILDERNESS ENCOUNTER
© 2018 **Susan Briggs Osborn**

All rights reserved. No portion of this book may be reproduced, stored in a retrieval system, or transmitted in any form or by any means—electronic, mechanical, photocopy, recording, scanning, or other—except for brief quotations in critical reviews or articles, without the prior written permission of the author.

ISBN-13: 978-1723434297

ISBN-10: 1723434299

Cover Design, Editing, and Publication by

Bene Vivere Publishing.

Foreword

This adventure trip, a three-credit elective course in college many years ago, encouraged me in my growth and development as a young Christian; a new, passionate believer in Jesus Christ. It provided me with a foundation with scripture as a source of authority and a pattern to start out my young life. The wilderness provided the setting for my further quest. My spirit and soul were nourished through outdoor experiences and meditation on God's world and His words!

In the last forty years as I have reflected upon this trip, this experience, I have often made reference to the lessons I learned there. At the prompting of a friend, I revisit them here. The greatest take-aways from the weeks spent in the wilderness were the development of a lifetime of enduring friendships, lasting relationships, how the role of leadership informed my beliefs concerning mentoring, and how I was astonished by love!

May 1978

"When existence is stripped to its barest essentials, the quest for reality and truth are simplified."

Francis Schaeffer

Well, I'm anxious to get started. We were set to leave Messiah College at 2:00 in the afternoon. It was 4:00 before we finally left the parking lot. I feel as if I have been captured. I am excited, but more than a little anxious about the unknown. The bus ride is bumpy as I write. Joyce and Rhoda were so sweet to me on the weekend. I appreciated that they waited with me until the bus pulled away. Such wonderful college friends. They were staying on working at the college for the summer.

Once we were down the road a short distance, Gilbert introduced himself as the Director of Ascend, Inc., a multi-faceted ministry to meet the needs of the whole man. The bus was filled with 30 of us college students, mostly Biology, Physical Education, or Recreation majors. Our seats were piled high with gear, and

1

with smiles on our faces, we were off on a wilderness experience.

This was to be a 21- day venture in conjunction with the college for 3 credits designed to build leadership through experience, high adventure through hard work, and to require skills of us that could help to build confidence. The emphasis was to look inward to self, outward to others, and upward to God. The purpose was also to draw individuals together by group living and sharing during team building exercises.

Karen was introduced as Gil's Assistant Director and a semi-professional canoeist and kayak instructor. We also met Doug who was in charge of the Urban Center, a unique ministry with delinquent youth that provides a year- long program to help young people and their families. All the programs are based on a Christian foundation, with the scriptures as the source of authority and the pattern for living. It is their belief that most lasting personal growth takes place under challenging, difficult, and stretching circumstances.

We also were introduced to a guy named Si and a logistics kinda' guy, Joe. The extensive wilderness areas of Virginia, West Virginia, North and South Carolina provide the setting for these growing experiences and they then were to become the stepping stones to self- awareness and self- respect.

I had done the physical, mental, and spiritual preparation that was suggested and was ready to feed my spirit and soul through meditation on God's world and Word. My desire was to develop and reconsider the claim of Jesus Christ on my life.

As we rumbled along for many miles, I made up my mind to stay open and not make judgments based upon outward appearances. We were instructed not to ask a lot of questions about our destination and details about daily destinations and upcoming events of the day. I began to think I would soon need to develop a greater ability to trust.

We were given bologna, salami, and cheese sandwiches. The drive was dreadfully long. The further we traveled, the greener it got. The "hills" were nice, and I thought of my college friend, Lindsey, from West Virginia who used to say of Pennsylvania's mountains "them thar' 'er jus' hills."

I've seen the welcome signs into Maryland, and Virginia, and we're almost through West Virginia. There seems to be a heightened sense of unity, and I think this is going to be fun.

Our first group effort, placing stones across this stream in West Virginia. "Stence" had it under control! A real "team" player!

We've stopped about five times. Seems a little too often to me. At one gas station they gave us tickets to a circus. We look like we are the circus; quite a conglomeration of people. We are in southern West Virginia, and the highway keeps winding and winding. We are off on a "cow path" spiraling higher and higher. I feel like we are going to fall off the edge with the bus listing to the side. I feel like we are in a boat with too many passengers on starboard. It doesn't seem like we could possibly go any higher. This is quite the ascent!

It's cold and dark now, and I am tired from riding in the cramped bus. Perhaps all the stops were for me to stretch my legs. I'm certain to learn patience on this trip. We've pulled into a wooded area and set up large tarps. I'll be next to Gil, Karen, and Wendy, and it looks like I'll be lying on the end and this rock in the middle of my back is not moving.

I've experienced my first miracle! I have never slept warmer or more comfortable than I did last night. It rained during the night, and I had difficulty winding down to sleep but it was long enough! Gil was the last to get up, so no hurrying anywhere on this first day! No watches, no clocks. Not sure what time it is.

The first activity of the day: pushing the bus. No information given, no questions asked.

We left civilization, not knowing for sure where or
when we would quit but with a great leader, Gil.
There were 15 of us, various majors and backgrounds,
mostly from Messiah College.

May 12th

It's cold and wet. Condensation has collected on our tarp. Packing for this trip was difficult for me. Folding clothes has not been my specialty. I am frustrated now as we are dividing the food and cooking utensils among ourselves. Everyone has been issued a metal canteen and a spoon. We each have food for four days even though it doesn't seem like it would sustain me for four hours. We have a sandwich bag that will hold our lunch each day for the week.

I thought that I was outgoing, but I'm feeling a little alienated from the group already. I'm going to try to get more involved tomorrow and be tolerant. I want to act like I'm confident, but I don't feel like I know very much about anything. I thought we'd have time together reading the Bible or praying together. I am realizing that I like to ask questions. I normally do. I don't like to find things out for myself. I prefer to be told what to do. They're giving us no idea or indication of what to expect from day to day. The group dallies, and then we hurry. Some are making scrambled eggs and bacon and some are building the fire. I guess I'll just be the reporter, the observer, at least for now. I don't want to miss a word. My thoughts are racing. I hope it warms up, so it dries up. I've taken my pack to the bus. It doesn't feel as heavy as much as it feels unbalanced. We haven't done much yet. I hope we have time to have devotions together soon. The eggs weren't bad at all, and I'm not crazy about eggs. Only about 4 or 5 tablespoons each.

It's late, I'm tired and wet. We hiked six miles today. I liked being in the front. I didn't feel any need to compete. I wanted to be in front so I could keep a steady and consistent pace. It's going to take a bit to stay together as a group with everyone walking at a different pace. We had to regroup several times. I get hot, and then I get cold. We crossed several streams. I find that I am off by myself, and I'm uncomfortable with this but I act like I'm shy, maybe it's intimidation or fear. I think too highly of myself. It's like I think I'm better than someone else, but I'm not quite sure what to do with this revelation or I'm unwilling to do something about it.

Betsy led us today. I'm developing a blister on the back of my heel already. I am aware of being independent, and I must not alienate myself from the group. I don't want that to happen. I like to be told what to do. I don't do well guessing, experimenting. Things are not always black and white, clear-cut, and straightforward. It's not ideal. I keep praying that I will "see" what I'm "supposed" to see, and that I'll not be disappointed. I'm waiting for the spiritual emphasis. Perhaps it doesn't come from talking about it. Hmmm…There's a thought!

It's raining, and we have to cross streams atop slippery rocks. I walked with Martha, a biology major, who works in the college kitchen. She knows wildflowers!

This was our first day. It was rainy and cool. The back packs were awkward.

We set up camp and got a fire going. We washed up at the last stop. Not likely to be much more civilization after this point as we're going into the deep woods! It is beautiful even in the rain.

I think we look like the characters, the raisins walking around all stiff-legged on the "Fruit of the Loom" commercial on television. We have plastic over our packs. It would have been a good investment to buy better "flys" to keep the rain off and from running down the plastic, soaking my back, and dripping down between my buttocks.

I'd like to be able to write better. I only have enough time to recall the events of the day now that we're hiking. I'm having difficulty expressing my feelings. I'm "all over the place." No stew left for me tonight, I took too much time trying to find hot chocolate in my pack. Everyone put a scoop in my canteen from theirs when they realized it. I'm not liking these feelings. I forget the many thoughts that run through my head during the day. It's hard to write in the rain, so I wait until I make a tent over my head with my light under my sleeping bag. I saw two whitetail deer along the trail and pollywogs in standing water.

We stopped so many times today. I'm anxious for a steady pace tomorrow. My pack is already disorganized and wet. "Lord, I love You. Teach me!"

"My soul thirsts for God,
For the Living God."
Psalm 42:2

May 16th

'm sitting near the raging brook. The rain has made the stream full and loud. I enjoyed rolling over in the night and hearing it rush across the rocks. Birds are singing this morning; looks like we may see some sunshine after all. It's still quiet and overcast though. I haven't figured out what time it might be. We're not rushing, but I'd like to get up earlier so I could get myself organized and have some time to read, write, and meditate. I think I'm supposed to be learning that my relationship to God is not to be confined, separated from my day, but part of my day. God is not far away or only in my ruminations about Him. I slept well. I was warm and comfortable. This is the greatest surprise. I'm refreshed, ready to go!

We had instant oatmeal and Jolene is organizing and preparing the meals. It had been four days since I was able to brush my teeth. I had a chance to get a little more organized, and I'm starting with a better attitude today.

Today has been a great day. It's not raining and warm: not hot and not cold. Martha is leading us today and the Appalachian Trail is easy walking, at least the section we did today. I'm enjoying the walking and the view is spectacular. I never thought I'd be overlooking the mountains of Virginia. I'm seeing my need to trust the Lord like I am trusting our leader to get us to the next food event! Gil is working to keep us moving together, in the right direction, safe, out of danger, and healthy. How much more should I need to trust in my Heavenly Father to lead me as I walk down the paths of life?

What I am learning most is to keep pace with the group. We are walking at different speeds. I function better going faster. It is difficult to hold myself back. I don't want to stop. It's hard to get going after we stop. I've been hiking up a storm. Betsy fell today. The ground was spongy, mushy. The only damage was that she got wet. The sun broke through the last six miles, but when we stop I get cold. The clouds are large, white, and puffy. My sweat is getting chilled. I've gotten the blisters on the ball of my foot bandaged.

The flapjacks were wonderful. They had honey and almond and coconut, and I don't know what else. I was hungry. We're in good spirits. Doug and Mike keep everything lighthearted and make us laugh. Doug comes up with some classic jokes. He is from New York

City and brings new light on everything that has ever passed through my brain. Mike keeps giving us exercise physiology lessons on ways in which flexibility increases strength. Jolene is a great help. We are in the Jefferson National Recreation Area. They have rerouted the Appalachian Trail extensively, so we are winding our way up and up. It doesn't seem like we could ascend much higher.

The birds are singing, and I'm happy and at peace. God is the song I sing. Beth and I talked. I mostly listened. She set a good pace. I was in the back of the group today. I feel better if I can move quicker, especially going up steep inclines. After a good break, I am raring to go!

We are at Iron Mountain Gap. This is a nice place now. I was so relieved that four or five people made the decision about our next destination. I am a follower, near the front now, not first but following close behind. I've been thinking about how Jesus had followers and about His leadership with the disciples.

We went through pastureland. It seemed strange to go through private property with animals around. It's a beautiful meadow. I don't suppose there are people other than hikers around. I can see what appears to be 15 mountain ranges. It was entertaining to watch

Karen crawl under the fence. I admire her. She moves so well. It doesn't hurt that she's got bright red hair and freckles and has asked if I'd room with her next semester.

PINE MOUNTAIN – 'logged off" in 1900.

We carried fence rails, anything we could find to make a fire. I thought I would never be able to get warm. I lost 18 pounds, and with the sweat from hiking I got so chilled, stiff and sore.

"I had fainted, unless I had believed to see the goodness of the Lord in the land of the living."
Psalm 27:13

We have been following a cow path and the elevation is about 3600 feet. We will be getting supper at 4800 feet. We are out of our way a couple miles, but the road was worth walking on. It is beautiful up here and the air is refreshing. I have been encouraged by Mike talking about the importance of seizing every opportunity to be clean and being certain to have a dry pair of socks, a dry hat, and warm clothes to sleep in. We have nine more miles to go before dark. It's going to be close. The last miles have been all up hill and rock. I'm exhausted. We pushed and pushed. I got ahead of the group and am rested now.

It's picturesque. I feel like I am in the middle of a Western movie. Pine Mountain looks like there should be Conestoga wagons, cowboys, and Indians. The gray rocks poke up from the earth in random piles. They say the fir and spruce were logged and burned off in 1900. Little shrubs abound. It feels like we walked into the past. A strange open feeling. Like John Wayne or something out of Gunsmoke or the wild west. We were walking up the dry creek bed. It was hot and dry and it cooled so quickly with the sun setting. The temperature dropped quickly.

Wendy was showing the first signs of hypothermia. Five students are in their sleeping bags already, and it is very cold. Feels like the desert at night. There are pieces of a dilapidated old barn that we have scavenged for firewood. No trees to get under tonight. We all got under one large tarp. It's so cold, and we're huddled so close. I had to climb up the hill a few times in the night. I kept sliding down the side of a rock. I washed my feet in the cold mountain stream and after dinner washed the chili pans.

The beginnings of hypothermia.

We got up and around and had a pancake. Another morning! It's going to be a warm one today. Mike has been so helpful on this trip. We went down the side of the mountain a little and carried back our packs full of wood. What a climb! The mountains are so beautiful. I couldn't ask for more. I am thinking about those first pioneers trekking through here. It feels like at any moment we'll see the Hatfield's and the McCoy's feuding.

Blue is the prominent color. The rocks are shades of blue and red and purple. It's breezy and there are horses and cattle trampling about. It doesn't seem like there would be enough for them to eat up here. I wonder how we can go even higher.

Our time of prayer and Bible reading was encouraging today. Gil read from Psalm 91, 103 and 104. I am encouraged to work with the group and help one another. There are small wildflowers around. The trail is like our lives. Sometimes we think we just can't continue, and we get weary. When we look back we can see what God has brought us through. If Gil would have pointed up to the top of this mountain when we started out and said we are going up there, I would have been discouraged and decided it was not possible. If I had known this was our destination I may have fallen before we started. I can see the wisdom now in not knowing what lies ahead. The second mile! When it is hot, and you feel like you can't go further it is best to keep on pushing. There is a passage in the Bible where it speaks of going beyond what is required of you. The law required they carry a burden at least a mile. The second mile is beyond the requirement.

I long to get to our destination, to sit and rest and to be warm and nourished. How much more are we to long for heaven? God has been preparing our place for thousands of years. I thought it would be good if I sought Jesus with the same intensity that I have sought this campsite. I look forward to my eternal home. I like this temporary one now however! We are at 5,000 feet and there is a spring, a cistern. Whoa! Cold water; instantaneous, muscle-cramping cold water.

We were given a 7- foot rope and had to get everyone over a high wall. There was no way under it, and it was too far to go around. We had a large log and our bodies. When we got almost everyone over, we decided to make a pyramid for the heavier one and the guys. Beth and I were on the bottom, and we got everyone over. Ernie led us well. He had a little too much help and encouragement in my opinion. I don't know how he didn't get frustrated with them. At least he showed no sign of it. I caught my foot. I couldn't quite get my leg over it. I held on to the log a little too long and had to try it again. Mike will lead us in the next hike to 5728 feet. We are at the last climb before we get to the highest peak. We are working well as a group.

Mount Rogers, 5,728 ft.

I am standing at the highest peak in Virginia on Mount Rogers. I can see Virginia, West Virginia, North and South Carolina, Tennessee, and nearly Georgia with field glasses. The mountains are hazy, hazy! If it were clearer, we would have trouble being too cold. The wind is quite cold. We are higher than Denver, CO. Karen took my picture, and this is my kind of place. Green-gardened paradise. Seems like heaven would be like this. The sun is shining through the pines. The air so fresh and smells so clean. Deep green hemlocks. The disciples would have been around Jesus in this type of solitude. God has brought me through. I love Him! It is rewarding to look back now. It's warm and peaceful, an excellent day.

The wildflowers remind me of Cora, a tennis camp counselor at Olmstead Manor in Ludlow, PA, before my mother died. The flowers are delicate and demonstrate the intricacies of God. Mike and I talked about the vastness of the world and yet how it seems so simple. Mike is a hometown kind of guy.

Karen and I talked about being roommates, our study habits and our routines. We enjoy being alone and finding a carrel in the library to study to block our view of what's going on. Talking made the time go quickly. Gil and Karen left for the night and left Doug to guide us to our destination in the morning. We will meet up with them at suppertime tomorrow.

I am glad to be alone and to meditate tonight. I got the wood and helped with packing up the utensils and cleaning pots and pans. I went down and brought up water, changed my clothes and got organized. I talked with Marty. She encourages me and inspires me. We got a raging fire going and later had macaroni and cheese with tuna fish and hot pink lemonade. You've not eaten well until you've tried this! We sang and talked around the fire. Marty said she has been experiencing loneliness, and Doreen talked about her need to ask others for help at times. Wendy is so sincere. I had misjudged her and asked God's forgiveness for being quietly critical of her without understanding. We talked about taking down barriers and defenses. I've been proud and independent. Beth played the harmonica under the starlit night!

May 18th

I didn't want to get up this morning. We stayed up later than usual. I didn't sleep well. I was so chilled. I laid on my arm and my shoulder and my hips stung against the ground. I didn't want to pop my head out from under my bag, but I couldn't breathe any longer. I had a much better attitude once I got to the stream and washed up. It was so cold outside, but the sun felt good and warmed me up. I brushed my teeth after breakfast and hot chocolate.

> The earth has music for those who listen.
> -William Shakespeare

It's going to be another beautiful day. I didn't even notice the hike. We have become so comfortable with one another, talking easily. It was enjoyable. Perfect hiking weather. The most comfortable of any day we have had. What a view. We are sitting on a peak, enjoying the view. Doug is leading the hike today. I looked around and nearly everyone is journaling. It's as if everyone has a fresh canvas. The view is stunning. Instantly the palettes and the ink are out.

We've made a steady climb to White Mountain and are resting now in Elk

Garden. Lunch is simple. We have been given the day to do whatever we'd like. I'm reading Proverbs again. We decided we'd hike a couple more miles to get to the peak of the mountain. We got to the top, and it's breathtakingly delightful to all my senses. I haven't encountered anything more lovely. There are mountains and valleys and more valleys and mountains. Such majesty. The temperature is moderate, perfectly comfortable.

We met Gil and Karen at the top. Gil had his large camera lens. When he points it at you it feels like you might be consumed by it, like it could suck you inside. There's a cabin up here. It is reminiscent of something that would have been used to hide someone in the throes of the Civil War.

The bus arrived, and we were done hiking and carrying large packs. The suspense of not knowing what we'll be doing next is incredible. It looks like we'll be doing rope work and perhaps rappelling. We have tied our tarps to the bus. Looks like a good night for sleeping. I think there is a quite a bit in store for us.

May 19th

'm looking forward to beginning a new week soon; especially, a new set of clean clothes! I've divided them into weeks, and it helps me to keep track of the days. I slept well and was comfortable. Beth gave me room. I was glad to be able to move.

The sun is shining, but the sky is gray. The fog is breaking up in the valley below us. The birds are singing even though it snowed here only three days ago. The wind is cold as it rushes through the pines. I'm ensconced on a large rock, one of my favorite places to perch, overlooking the valley. The crows are making a fuss about something. We are just waiting for breakfast. I offered to help, but it is not necessary for all of us to help since the job is not that big this morning.

I've been reading the Bible and praying. I want to follow whatever God has for me and listen for His voice, His leading. I combed my hair. It is a minor frustration getting it to cooperate. I had a pleasant dream with Joyce about Joyce. She was happy and smiling. That's what I remember! I dreamed also of my brother

Rusty, and it was in astonishing color. Simple pleasures!

A big breakfast! Wow! I had three or four pancakes, eggs, and sausage…Mmmm! So filling! I put it all together in the canteen, on top of each other and poured syrup over the top!

The wind is blowing fast. I've never been in wind whipping around at this speed.
Strange. The clouds are whizzing by. It is like billowing smoke. The cloud shadows are ripping across the mountains. It is so bright now and clear.

> **Let nature be your teacher....**
>
> **-William Wordsworth**

I was the first one to climb. I got the rope tied on and climbed up a 60 feet slick rock wall. I used my knees some. The rock feels quite rough through my pant leg. My grips and fingertips were raw. I couldn't feel whether I had a good grip. Some of the time I did not and almost lost my breath as I realized I was dangling in air. I got a little twisted and the rope was rubbing some against my neck. I finally got in a crack, got a good hold, and I was able to get up. My legs were shaking and quivering. I don't think I'll forget the feeling in my legs of the total lack of glycogen reserve. Pure exhaustion of the muscles. I could not control or stop them from shaking. It didn't seem there was anywhere I could possibly grab a hand-hold. The team was shouting directions to me and giving me instructions of what I might do. It was only a frustrating clamor of noises by the time it got to me.

I so enjoyed the rappelling. It was especially freeing once I realized I had full control of the rope. When I relaxed and realized I could put my weight back and "hop" around, it was fun! I liked being the first one and then relaxing and observing the rest coming down. I am so tired though. I got a candy bar, a Baby Ruth, an orange and a piece of honey bread! I've not been losing weight yet. I'm certain I will, but not yet.

After everyone completed their climb and rappelling, we went on a trust walk. We were blindfolded while Gil gave the group instructions to hold onto the back of one another's shoulders. We followed a rope and Lorraine led us blindfolded. She gave directions to the person behind her and then the person behind her to the person behind them, all in a line together. We went up hills, over rocks, and around trees. I was a little anxious. I was even nervous some. When we took our blindfolds off we were amazed at the distance we had covered and the way the rope curved around and around. The dynamics were funny. The people in the back got the messages earlier than the time they need to correct their motions and then were unprepared when they needed to be changing their motions. It must have looked hilarious seeing us ducking and weaving under and around branches when it wasn't necessary at that time and then watching us smack into branches. No one was hurt. We moved so slowly.

When we were finished with the trust walk, we got garbage bags and picked up trash. It is difficult to believe that in this setting that people could have dumped garbage over the sides of the mountains. Perhaps the wind or falling rock pushed and pulled it around, but it looked like it was dumped. We picked up bag after bag and didn't seem to diminish the piles. Disheartening. Seems like this is the last place anyone would want to do that. Perhaps their packs were too full, too heavy, and they had no way to pack it out. My brain was trying to find a way to excuse this humanity.

I decided to organize trash "walks" for my college group/club and back home too. I wanted to be angry at people and their behavior. It was difficult for me to comprehend this kind of action. Even if they weren't godly or ethical, I found it hard to understand the lack of respect for the environment for nature, for the beauty out here.

It's warm, but the breeze is cold. I moved to the clearing and to spots on the ground where the clouds were not making shadows so I could warm myself with the sun. It's only 3:00 or 4:00, and we will be able to climb and rappel again before dark on a higher cliff. I am up for the challenge!

Thinking of Oz today. I am looking forward to sharing with him. I am praying for our future together. I find it difficult that he could love me. I am afraid of losing it before I know it is secured. Strange.

Betsy lost her footing, slipped down in a crevice, and got her foot stuck. It looked like something to laugh about initially. Once she realized her situation though, she began to be afraid and began crying. We were helpless on lookers as she tried to free herself from the awkward angle of her foot in the crack. We were nervous for her. She was scared, and we were all relieved when she managed to pull and twist away.

Wendy didn't want to climb. I made a conscious effort to look around at the view when I was up there during my attempt. A breathtaking view! Lovely to see at such a height. Ernie and Mike were giddy like little boys. They were referring to one another as Robert Redford and

Paul Newman. Beth and I ran to get a better view to take a picture of the sunset over the pines. She twisted her ankle and pulled a muscle. She says it happens often. I remember her having it taped during basketball practices. She was thrashing in pain, and I felt bad for her. She didn't want my help. There wasn't anything I could do for her, but I continued to feel badly about it when I'd awaken in the night. We missed the sunset and a quiet dinner and our excitement and communication were lessened.

Karen and I talked about being roomies. She talked about Norman and her summer job. She's going to be at about 9,000 feet in Arizona as a Wilderness Director. We talked about how independent we are and whether it's the correct posture, if it is okay to like to be alone.

We ate baked beans, mashed potatoes, and green beans. Karen is not too happy with me for not eating veggies. We saw 8 canoes coming up the mountain on a truck. Seemed strange at this elevation. It was humorous how Karen tried to convince us that it didn't mean we were going to begin canoeing. There's no water here, but she was trying to convince us that we weren't going canoeing! Ha! What a cover up! We were supposed to hike to the canoes tomorrow, but it looks like they have come to us! I had hoped to climb again, but when Mike said he was exhausted and Ernie fell 30 feet, I decided I didn't need to fit it in tonight. I need to relieve myself. Lorraine is telling jokes, and I'm nearly ready to pee my pants.

It has been so good to read Joyce's letter over and over again. I think a lot about her and particularly wonder what she's doing now. I want to rip off two or three pieces of paper and write to her. I feel still really hurt about my relationship with Louise, and I want to write to her. It's getting dark and cold and I want every minute of writing light possible. I've got to stay on top of this experience and really let the Holy Spirit speak to me. "Create in me a clean heart, O God, and renew a steadfast (right) spirit within me." Psalm 51.

I think the wind is going to blow right through my tent. Oh, Jesus, I need you. I am really seeing my inadequacy. I don't know what kind of trees these are all around me, but they have beautiful white blossoms. They smell a little bit, but anything smells good. The winds are changing, and I'm wondering what to do. I don't want to get this way so soon. I've got to hang on and enjoy this. I've got to let the Lord minister to me. It's good to hear the stream flowing, but not the thunder. I don't know the time; the solitude is kind of nice. I used oak leaves as toilet paper.

Wow! I can't believe I'm actually here doing this. It will be a time of much retrospection. I had no real intentions of coming on Wilderness Encounter until I paid my final money. That's strange. I shoot for too small. I must work on my self-image. The Lord can and wants to do much more in me. Thank you for your peace and joy.

I can remember that at the beginning of the school year, my freshman year in college, I cried out to God for a friend. It seemed every day I cried out and earnestly sought the Lord for a friend. I want you to know, Joyce, that you are God's prayer answered. You are the very person that God sent to be my friend, and I know that with all my being.

I've been talking to the Lord for about an hour. The Holy Spirit has really been speaking to me. I know that God is here. He has promised to take complete care of me. I have gone to the bathroom four or five times, and I've only been here for half a day. This is unusual. The Lord has promised good for me. There is an awful lot of light left. It must have been much earlier than I thought. I've just been talking to my Lord alone out here. I heard a few crows fly by and watched a colony of ants. They are miraculous.

The Lord told me He wants to use every circumstance and situation in life to teach me that

I am not self-sufficient. Praise Him! I can't even write down all I'm feeling. I'm just having such free and open fellowship and communion with my Father. He is very real to me now. I keep hearing it in my mind: "This is only a beginning; this is only a very small portion of what I have for you." It all comes down to Jesus and me. In my spiritual relationship, I cannot look to any of my friends, family, or loved ones. It is a relationship between Jesus Christ the King and Susan. It has to be the both of us.

May 20th

Saturday-We woke up early this morning. It was nice to see the sun shining. We packed everything into MacDonald's bright orange drink coolers (igloo-like juice containers) and plastic 5- gallon pickle jugs. We rode eating granola bars on the way.

As we traveled along the rugged roads, it looked like folks were living in rough living conditions. The cabins were poor condition up here. There was a small school with maybe five rooms. Some of these homes made me feel like my house is a mansion.

We are headed into another state. North Carolina, I think, and we've arrived at a river. My canoeing partner is Doug. The pines along the river banks are very aromatic and fragrant. I got nervous last night as my pen ran out of ink. Luckily for me, Betsy lent me hers!

May 21st

THE river is moving at about 2 ½ miles an hour. We stopped for lunch in a pasture with cattle looking on. We had cheese and crackers. We went on at a leisurely pace, and it was a beautiful view. Paddling never got boring as we watched for rocks and rapids which demanded my attention.

Jolene is our leader today, and we stopped at a fresh running spring and rested. The sun is setting. We decided to put our tarps up as it looks like it may rain. Lorraine, Betsy, and Doug are already sleeping around me. We went to bed early. I heard the rain pitter patting on the tarp and then pounding above my head.

Simultaneously, I heard five or six others groan with me. I had visions of my things being ruined and of spending the day drenched with river water underneath us and frigid rain water above us all day.

When I woke up, I heard the pleasant chirping and singing of birds persisting with their melodies now! The day is wonderfully warm and the sun dances in glitter on the river. Martha

A peaceful, quiet place after a long and hot day. I sensed the presence of God so strongly upon a "Rock."

gave me a back massage. It was relaxing, and I was ready to sleep. Some of the girls were already friends before the trip so it is sometimes tricky to develop a closer friendship with those you don't already know because they are sometimes paired. I'm happy and I'm enjoying the trip immensely. I'd hate if the group got into cliques. We've been together long enough.We're surviving well. I've got plenty of food, plenty of exercise, and I have a close relationship with God.

We had ravioli last night for dinner and oatmeal for breakfast this morning. Karen and Si are skilled at canoeing and everyone seems to be doing well. The warm sun greeted us, and we are ready to begin our second day of canoeing.

It's Sunday, and we will sing and have a worship service today. I've been thinking of Dennis and Bonnie and my friend Tammy, how they enjoy loving Jesus.

We've completed another day on the river. It is nice to sit and relax and reflect on yet another day. I'm sitting on a large rock under a hemlock. I'm looking over the New River, gathering my thoughts. I led the group today. I'm certainly not a leader. I didn't feel confident reading the river map. We were down the river a mile or two and came upon a dam. We pulled over to the left side along the bank and carried the canoes around. It took about a half an hour. It wasn't too bad, we stopped and had some protein snack, a mix of M and M's, nuts, sesame and sunflower seeds, chocolate chips, and sour balls. I finished my handful, half a mile down the river. We went 2 or 3 more miles down the river and under a low bridge. North Carolina is beautiful. We crossed again over into Virginia. The river meanders back and forth between the two. We had peanut butter and crackers, and Si talked to us about entering the rapids. We approached them, and I thought "well, here goes!" Doug and I got hung up on some rocks immediately. I panicked a little and wasn't sure what to do. I got out and turned us and we were alright for a while. It was fun, exciting, and challenging.

We did much better on the second layer of rapids. Doug was patient in maneuvering us. We kept paddling and bouncing up and down doing fine, and I remember hitting some big waves. The water on me felt so good. I remember the excitement I felt, something I assumed it would feel like riding a bucking bronco. The boat filled up with water, and we hit a large solid rock and then another. The boat filled up some more and spun, and we hit another big rock. The boat flipped over, and I held onto the paddle and the Ensolite pads. I remember that my knees hit rocks on the bottom and caused pain on my shins and feet.

The canoe began to carry me down stream, and I remember hearing Doug yell to stay behind the tip. I saw Si and Wendy tipped over also, which surprised me. Mike and Karen were off to the side helping people out. I must have bailed water for an hour after I got it tipped up, steadied, and under control. I was not scared out of my mind as I thought I would be. I enjoyed it. It was invigorating, though I wondered why I couldn't have conquered it like the other five.

We rested on the bank, while we recovered and made sure everyone was all right. Doug and I lost the extra paddle we had, and Wendy lost her socks. I'm bruised, but fine. Karen and Stence got hung up, and Karen said she was under the canoe while it was revolving. A true hydraulic. She'll have a story to tell Norman. It's a bright sunny day. I got a little sunburn. It's not painful, and I think I'll tan. I am frustrated with my job as a leader. Today was tough. It was difficult.

I got us to our destination spot though, and it didn't look good for camping in my opinion. Mike and Ernie looked around for nearly an hour for some place better. I found a decision difficult. I didn't want to be wrong or make a mistake. The few I did make, I changed. When I finally make a decision, I need to stick to it and not be swayed. I have such a fear of failure.

Finally, Mike, Ernie, and I decided to continue. We went a few hundred feet and found a nice spot with a fresh stream. I was content, it was level and beautifully-wooded.

We quit early. It was 3:00 which gave us time to beach our boats, build a fire, set up the tarps and swim in the river with our soap! I appreciated the water tonight.

Beth, Doreen, Jolene, Martha, and I put on our life preservers and let the river take us away! It was refreshing. I lathered up and feel fantastic! We're having tuna noodle casserole. It is calm and peaceful. The sound of the river bouncing over the rocks is soothing. Si said he has never had a more fun -loving group than ours. I think he was sincere! One week to go!

May 22nd

I t's a nice morning. I slept well. I woke up at Lorraine's feet. I guess I kept digging in my sleeping back deeper and deeper until I was at the bottom. I had some awake time. I thought of being home and how much work I need to do this summer. I need to get moving and it's going to be rough.

I want to finish the week strong. I didn't want to get on the water today. As my thoughts turned to the natural scenic beauty I felt better about the day as it went on. I thought of my friends from home and how I would describe this trip and how much it has allowed me, even encouraged me to change. I wondered how I might explain that to them. I hope it is evident. I think Oz will be a bigger and bigger part of my life. I want him to be. I'm a little anxious about what the future may bring, but I am trusting God to lead me.

For breakfast I had an English muffin with honey and peanut butter. We are running late. I heard a crow outside of my tent cawing incessantly.

Today was a battle. I couldn't keep myself present. I began to think about going home, a strange shift. I didn't want to canoe. Seems like we are far from anywhere. We went three miles and took a break. I am exhausted and tired of sitting in the canoe. I don't care if I ever see a canoe again. I've been working and straining hard. I am frustrated with my partner. I feel as if we are working against one another. It's likely that I am the problem. I've been thinking of the verse, "regard one another as more important than yourself."

Ernie was sure he could throw a stone across the river. He walked across, almost to the other side before he managed to do it.

We had some trail mix for a snack. I've had enough of that! I thought lunch would never come! My shoulders and arms are tired, the muscles are burning from strain. I'm more uncomfortable than at any other time since we started. My shoulders hurt. There are only so many things one can do with their knees in a canoe. I felt cramped and the sun was scorching. I wanted to jump in the water. We tried to throw stones across for about 15 minutes. We sat in the middle of the river watching the sun go down. No more current.

> Wilderness is not a luxury but a necessity of the human spirit.
>
> -Edward Abbey

We got our gloves, boots and gear together and went on a ropes course. The rope was strung along 10 or 15 pines about 7 feet high and with a rope about 6 feet above that. We used the top rope as a guide line and walked on the lower one, keeping our balance as we moved up a sloped rope. I went second. I found it extremely exciting. It was fun and a challenge. I would like to do it again sometime. It was good to hear everyone encouraging one another. We were "spotting" each other. The guys were helpful and encouraging. I felt like we were supporting one another.

Karen cut her wrist preparing dinner and didn't get upset with the bloody cut. She is calm and has a good head on her shoulders. Gil took Karen to the closest civilization to call an ambulance and to take her to the hospital. Everyone handled the situation well, and we continued with our rope course.

I chatted with Beth and Doreen and Betsy. Betsy has a good sense of humor. Her attitude toward herself is improving. Wendy amazes me. I took her picture, and she was expressive. Si and Joe took Jolene, Stence, Betsy, and Wendy rappelling. Wendy said it was easy and enjoyable. Stence really liked it, so I'm encouraged.

I helped a little in preparing the potatoes and chicken. I can't believe the way they are feeding us. This is not stressful yet. I guess I build things up to be so big and bad, and then I'm relieved when it's not that bad. I guess I thought the trip was going to be very difficult. It hasn't been yet. I'm finding it extremely enjoyable. I'm amazed at how calm and well Karen handled being cut. I'm just praying for the Lord's peace upon them. She's gonna' need some stitches, I'm looking forward to seeing how things worked out.

Jolene got pretty burnt today. We are getting ready for our best meal yet. Jolene really enjoyed rappelling too. I can't believe this day. It seems like the sun is never going to go down. I don't mind though. Each day gets better and better. The Lord is so good.

Boy, it is so nice! The sun is shining, and the mountains are so beautiful. I took my turn rappelling. It was a lot of fun on a very small scale, but we will be doing more. Si and Joe are knowledgeable, and it is interesting to listen to their experiences and understanding of rappelling. I'm very interested in knowing more, but it can become too technical. I hope to be able to do it again someday. It is just climbing down a hill backwards and knowing how much rope to let out. It is very safe. There are several types of knots one needs to know to tie the seat that holds you. I'll be eager to do more tomorrow. Si said there is an awful lot of accomplishment in getting up to a peak or down the side of the wall. He said that everyone has their Everest.

I'm really content tonight; it has been a tremendous day. I can parallel Si (as the belayer), and Christ as my stronghold. The belayer is the one who is responsible for your safety in rappelling. Jesus is my belayer! He holds the reins that control the path of my life, and I need to trust in Him completely.

We had an excellent meal: chicken, baked potatoes, corn, and a pear. It was good over the fire.

Karen and Gil returned; Karen got three stitches. You wouldn't be able to tell. She's calm and back in the swing. She's going to go rappelling tonight before it gets dark. Doreen and Beth, Mike and Jolene went to get water.

I need to go at God's pace and learn to work with the group and go at another's pace. I need to learn to trust God a day at a time rather than three years ahead. I did some thinking today, and I was confused about what God wants of me and what He wants me to learn. I thought of Oz today, and I keep committing my relationship with him to God. I want it to be good and what God desires.

We talked around the fire last night about Wilderness Encounter being a place where we could draw nearer to God, like a "mountaintop experience." We need to seek Him as fervently and intensely in our everyday lives as in a situation where we are away from people and close to nature. He desires that we are close to Him and seek Him and to be sensitive to His Spirit and to other people. I want to learn and

"I will lift up my eyes to the hills from where my help comes."
Psalm 121:1

remember this experience as one that I could make applicable to my life in the years to come.

Si, Joe, Gil, and Karen are in leadership. Si seemed like a smart aleck kid. My first impressions couldn't have been more wrong. I am judgmental. He is so sweet. He has a good ability as a teacher. I don't know Joe well. He is an encourager, a funny guy. I wondered about Gil's strength as a believer, how His faith would be demonstrated. I can see now how strong he is spiritually. He is patient and understanding. I like his perspective. Karen is strong; not much can happen that she won't believe and trust in God.

> In the presence of nature, a wild delight runs through the man in spite of real sorrows.
>
> -Ralph Waldo Emerson

Doug is a unique man that God wants to train as a leader in the Wilderness Program. He's a former drug user from the streets of Chicago. He is happy go lucky and trusts the Lord. He explained that if God wants him to live the camp life that he would do it. He is confident that God can change him into being more helpful than he has been in the past. He spoke of how terrible his life had been and that now his days are new. He is thrilled so far with the experiences of this trip which is not one that he would be able to get while living in the city.

I have been shy with the others, but I found myself warming to Marty's pleasant demeanor. She said she feels a need for people. She is outgoing and energetic. I thought at first that I wanted to avoid her. Mike is polite, mannerly, and he seems like a nice guy. He is a work horse. He was so thrilled today to have clean hair and to be able to wash up with the refreshing water. He's the big, muscular guy I had to pull off the bottom of the 13' pool for my Lifeguarding test.

Ernie is sensitive to other's needs. I respect Ernie. He was one of the first students I was introduced to when arriving at college. He has a healthy appetite with a high metabolism. He can be concerned sometimes about not having enough food, but we probably have plenty. He is the kind of guy that wouldn't ask for anything and especially any special treatment.

Doreen is quiet around me. I don't know her well. I'm not comfortable around Beth. I enjoy her company. She is reserved, reticent. Wendy throws me all kinds of curveballs. Just when I think I have her defined, she reinvents herself. Most intriguing. She is open and honest and eager to learn more about God. She requests that we sing Amazing Grace and

Amazing Love, How Can It Be? And Can it Be, hymn #209!

I am anxious to know Karen. We have some things in common. She loves aloneness and independence and is realizing she does need people. She works hard. If people will lead and take charge, then she is glad to follow and let them do as much as they'd like. She seems sometimes like she doesn't care, but she is not apathetic.

Jolene has helped me. I feel like I have benefitted from knowing her. She speaks so vibrantly of God's love. She is good at expounding on the goodness of God. Her love for God is so evident.

Such a variety of wildflowers around us. I am so grateful to Martha for telling us the names of many of them. I thought I would like to get a book about the flowers when I get home.

Ernie and I talked about school and especially leadership scholarships. He has some great ideas. I'm sure he will be successful in his pursuits.

I'd like to get to know Betsy better. She seems to be eager to learn and understand more of what God is revealing to her. She is often in the rear when we hike, and she says she is exhausted. She is surprised because she said she trained and prepared extensively for the trip. She runs cross country, but she said she is in pain. She talks about how difficult and deeply humbling it has been to be in the back, but that she is learning some valuable lessons about herself.

Lorraine intrigues me. She reminds me of a little lamb. She is so delicate, soft, and tender-hearted. I enjoy her company. She is full of life, energy, vitality! She will be the Resident Assistant on our floor next semester. This will be so fun!

We had some time to share with one another as we talked around the fire. Gil wanted some feedback on some of our reactions about what it has been like, not knowing where or what our itinerary is from day-to-day. I shared that I was aware that God wants us to depend on Him daily, moment-to-moment, step-by-step trusting in Him. If we can trust in people and in a rope that we are dangling from, how much more can we trust our God? It has been wonderful seeing the group mature, and I enjoyed hearing about each other's expressions of faith. We did some singing and drank of the beauty of our natural surroundings. Just wonderful! We cannot limit

Him. We have been so aware of His being with us.

May 25th SOLO

I knew from the description of this college course that it was to include some elements of climbing, canoeing, rappelling, running, a solo time, and team building exercises. We were not given details except to aid and prepare us in our physical training and in the few items we were to bring. We did not know the sequence or the details of these activities. We were told not to take our Bibles with us but to choose some verses that we could mediate on and that would be a comfort to us if we were to be alone for several hours. The verses I chose were Galatians 2:20 "I have been crucified with Christ and I no longer live, but Christ lives in me. The life I now live in the body, I live by faith in the Son of God, who loved me and gave himself for me." Another verse was from Psalm 51: "Create in me, Oh God, a clean heart, and renew in me a right spirit. Restore unto me the joy of my salvation and take not your Holy Spirit from me."

We were each given a tarp, three matches, and we could take our sleeping bag, canteen, and our verses. We began walking and every quarter mile or so we were each assigned a spot, a place where we were to enjoy the outdoors, the virgin earth. We were allotted ten paces to our right and ten paces to our left along a stream for water and where we were to stay until the leaders came for us, presumably days later.

It is really a beautiful day. The sun is shining brightly upon my back. There is a slight calm, soothing breeze that blows across my arms. I went to sleep last night when I could no longer see—probably between 9:30 p.m. and 10 p.m.—and got up around that time this morning. That's a whole lot of sleep for me and probably for anyone. I think of how it must have been in earlier times with no electricity. They went to bed when it got dark and got up as soon as the sun awakened them. They did not have the things we do to close out the day. We are pretty much night people. We do an awful lot at night. It is a rare individual who likes to rise early, believe me. Oh, I see things so much differently in the morning. I don't mind being alone in the morning at all.

The Lord spoke to me telling me what a privilege and an honor to have this time alone with Him. When in my life am I ever again going to have three days to spend doing nothing but talking, praying, and listening to God? Probably never. I'm completely alone. I can't hide from God or run away this time because there is nowhere to run or no one to whom to run. The Lord showed me how many times I run to my journal. Many times I resort to people, or reading, or anything I find to do to get away from that personal one-to-one talk with God. He is longing to be my friend and to have a conversation with me as any other person would. He is a personal God. He wants to show me the reality of Himself. I went down to the road and piled my rocks.

"...my tongue is the pen of a ready writer."
Psalm 45:1

I have a very poor sense of direction, and I don't know really if I piled the right rocks. I don't have much distance to the right or left of me, and I don't want to get too close to anyone else. I know where they are, and that kind of bothers me. I lay awake probably for an hour or so. It was good not to have to get out of my sleeping bag for anything. I kept thinking to myself that the longer time there, the less time I had to worry about occupying. The Lord promised me that I would be dry and warm, and He did not fail me. I went to sleep exactly when He told me to, and I didn't wake up but once. I looked at the moon; it was so bright. Oh, the joy that flooded my soul when first I opened my eyes. I was warm, comfortable, alive, and well. Nothing I know surpasses that comforting, peaceful feeling of waking up alive, healthy, and in love with the Master of all creation. That is one experience in my life that I find difficult to capture.

I went to the stream and sat for a time. I just watched the water. I tried to understand how it came across the rocks as it does and wondered why it took certain patterns. I was afraid to sit beside the stream for long because it was so reflective. I thought it might cause me to delve deep within myself, and I didn't feel like I wanted to do that yet this morning. There was a snail attached to the bottom of my tent near my head. The Lord taught me a bit about myself through that snail. I picked it up and threw it away from my tent. Boy, how many times I cast aside things that I don't like, things that are unpleasant, and things that I don't want to deal with. I must not be that impatient and control my life to that extent.

I see how the Lord wants to speak to me through EVERYTHING! He wants complete control of <u>every</u> situation, circumstance, moment, and <u>feeling</u>. He knows me. He knows EVERYTHING about me. He knows how I react. He knows how I think and feel. He knows ME. The stream just flows and flows incessantly. I wondered how the rocks could possibly endure being hit with that falling water century after century. Then I realized that they had to be broken, crushed, molded, shaped, formed, and reformed by the water. Lord, I want to be yielded and broken before you.

Well, for breakfast I had a pint of water and for lunch another pint of water. The Lord has promised me that my system will get back to normal with no problems as soon as I get done here. I guess I'm kind of looking forward to going back and sharing with everyone. The way my body functions is very interesting to me. I feel like I have lost a few pounds. I feel a little lean, but I feel comfortable. My back is tight and has quite a hunch to it. I'm sure I see a little bit of tan. I've got two little bites on my wrist or they might be poison ivy spots or something poisonous. I wonder if all these bugs on me and around me are because I'm very dirty. I sure don't like the thought of that.

I was lying in the sun, but the bugs were crawling all over me and the flies were bothering me. I figured the sun was draining me of a lot of fluid and energy, so I went and sat down by the stream. I'm amazed at how close my thoughts are to me. I sat on a rock and just let the water fill my canteen up over and over again. The Lord really showed me some parallels. That stream never stops, and it never runs out of water. How much like Jesus that is. I could keep putting my cup in there as much as I wanted to drink. So it is with the Lord.

I was just sitting and lingering by the stream for probably half an hour. I kept saying in my mind: "You can't sit still; you've got things you should be doing and places you should be going." No way! It is okay for me to sit here all day and think of Him. That's what He wants me to do—meditate on Him all day. I have to delight in this. I must delight myself in Him. It seems like I have longed for times to be alone with Him, and here I am trying to find other things to do. Look at this privilege. I'll probably never get the chance to be this alone with Him again. The water is so abundant and just flows and flows. Each rock makes the course of the stream as each individual person makes up the Body of Christ—the course of Christ to the world. When one stone is moved or altered, the whole course of the stream is shifted. That's kind of like the verse where if one member of the body hurts, we all hurt; if one member weeps, we all weep, if one member is joyful, we are all joyful. I sure hope this isn't taken out of context too much.

The stream is kind of like my life. It moves along (the stream) never stopping (eternal life) and there are many obstacles and rocks (trials, tribulations, lessons, etc.). The stream has something that my life kind of lacks, though, and that is the ability to flow over those rocks smoothly and to make new paths, new streams, when its course is changed. When I moved a rock, the stream just wound around and found a new course without stopping or hesitating. When I dammed it up, the stream found another means of flowing. I need to be like that—able to continue to flow regardless of the rocks. That analogy definitely has some leaks, but it showed me a lot.

> There are moments when all anxiety and stated toil are becalmed in the infinite leisure and repose of nature.
>
> -Henry David Thoreau

Also, the Lord spoke to me about being an individual—a unique individual, but yet similar to others so that I could be compatible. He showed me that I am an individual--a rock among many rocks and yet I make up the course of the stream. He showed me that I have unique friendships, but yet some are similar so I can relate and be integrated. He showed me that I have unique friendships and yet they are similar so I can learn to love. I love in different ways. He showed me the possibility and the beauty in a relationship between a woman and a woman, and He said that it was good. He meant for it to be. I thought of the many relationships that I have like that—Joyce, Ro, Karen, Coleen, Dana. He also showed me the unique relationship between a man and a woman (not physically or sexually). I thought about my relationships with Ron, Don, Myron, Tito, Chris, and Roy; I know that they are also good. It seems much more difficult for me, though. The Lord showed me that there is a very real possibility and reality for me to have a physical, sexual relationship with a man. That is extremely difficult for me to comprehend and understand. I must begin to learn of that kind of relationship. It scares me because I know little of it, but I feel like there is a real possibility in this type of relationship between Oz and me. The Lord showed me that it can be the most beautiful and tremendous experience if I will let it be pure. Oh, how much I want that relationship to be pure.

A grouse flew by; it startled me. I watched an ant carrying an inchworm and another ant carrying a stick. I really wonder where that ant gets all that strength. I'm just so aware of my thoughts that I can do nothing else but write. It's hard to believe that there is nothing to do but <u>SO</u> much to do. I'm definitely not bored. I am really overwhelmed at the closeness that Jesus wants me to have with Him. He wants me to meditate upon His Word and upon Himself. This is really new.

The dogwood trees are so beautiful in bloom. They are what I didn't know before. They have a pinkish white blossom, and the aroma is very nice. The sun is really warm upon me. It is a magnificent day. It is very difficult to keep my mind on one thing—as one might be able to tell when reading this. The aroma in the breeze is so sweet. I just cut a young pine, and the aroma is so good. The sap oozes from its layers. I watched a blue jay; I'm curious to see how it lives. It is a big one. A white-tailed deer startled me also. It was large, and it snorted very loudly. It sounded as if someone blew his or her nose. I can still hear it off in the distance. I wrote a letter to Joyce and thought about the Lord. It is so nice to have the sun on my back. I read this journal and am amazed at what the Lord has done in the last 12 days.

The sun is going down now. It is about suppertime. I need to get some water. I guess I'm really not very hungry. I've stretched my stomach pretty well with water. The hardest part for me is after the sun goes down. Today went quickly, though, and I'm really glad about that. This entire trip has gone fast now that I look and see that it is almost over. There is so much more I know that the Lord wants to speak to me about. I am amazed at how quickly this day has gone. I am really very happy. I think that I am mentally exhausted. Because I haven't done anything but write all day, my body feels kind of weak—almost like it is deteriorating.

The Lord gave me a song while at the stream:

I'm not alone, I'm not alone,
I'm not alone, I'm not alone.
You are my joy, You are my life, You
are my peace, You are my calm, You
are my joy, You are my song. I'm not
alone, I'm not alone, I'm not alone, I'm
not alone.
You are my friend, You are my love,
You are my hope, You are my song.
When I'm afraid, You are my strength,
when I am cold, You are my warmth,
when I am lost, You are my path. I'm
not alone, I'm not alone, You are my
stream, You are my life.

I thought today I would gather firewood and dig a hole, but the Lord promised to keep me dry and warm. I have no need for a fire. He is my consuming flame. I have just gone through the most humbling experience of my life. This morning I put my rocks in the wrong place. I lost my sense of direction. Gil and Karen came up to see if I was okay. Wow! Did I blow it! I felt like I had ruined the whole experience and purpose of solo. I told them I was okay, so tonight I went straight down from my tent and put a big S with my rocks.

I don't know what happened, but I got terribly lost. I lost all sense of direction and couldn't find my way back to my spot. I panicked and ran in all different directions. I walked and walked, stopped and tried to find my direction, then ran and panicked some more. I must have walked and run about two miles. I kept getting further and further lost. The sun was going down fast, and I kept praying that no one would see me. I didn't even have my whistle. I finally found the road after about an hour. I walked down it to the end. Then I walked up it and guess who I ran into about a mile down the road? Gil and Karen. Oh, God! I wanted to cry so much. I put my head down and walked slowly toward them. I was so upset and sweating so much. I kept saying how upset I was, but I didn't want Gil to know how lost I was. Oh, my pride. I didn't want to look at him.

He showed me how far off I was. I couldn't believe it. He showed me how to get to my spot and said my difficulty was that the road and the creek curved. The angle of my tent was the opposite. I felt so much like a fool, and he told me to calm down and let the Lord teach me. I felt like I had ruined the whole purpose of solo. I wanted no contact with people and here twice in one day I saw Karen and Gil. Gil was so understanding. He kept telling me to let the Lord teach me. Oh, my pride. I condemned myself so much, and I know it was of Satan. I hugged Gil, said I was sorry, and turned my back. I couldn't look at him.

I came back and cried like a baby. Oh, how I cried. I felt like I had disappointed God and ruined my solo, but God showed me that it's okay to cry and also to make mistakes. He showed me that I'm going to make many mistakes and lose my direction often in my life. I am also going to get lost, panic, go the other direction, fail, and fall down a lot. However, God is never going to leave me and never going to condemn me. He's going to pick me up and point me back to my tent. He wants me to take every situation, every failing, every falling and stumbling, and every loss of direction and let Him work through that to teach me. He wants to use every one of my mistakes to teach me. He wants me to learn from every experience, every situation, and every trial I go through. He can use my blunders to teach me so many important lessons. Oh, this hurts so badly. My pride is really being put down, and I must cry out to God. Thank you for teaching me, Jesus. I am mentally exhausted, and I got my physical workout for today. There is just enough light to write to Tammy and Louise.

May 26th

I am not sleeping very well. I heard deer snorting all through the night. The whippoorwills are so loud and consistent that the sound caused a pounding rhythm in my head. I hear all kinds of night sounds. The moon is very bright. I'm exhausted and thinking so much that it's hard to sleep. I awakened before the sun, set up my rocks, and felt pretty weak. I'm slightly hungry, so I drank some water. I watched a deer come right up to my tent. He was smaller than the one I saw last night. I watched him closely as he ate; he was not aware of me. I liked that. I meditated on some scripture and started a letter to Tammy.

I couldn't believe that Karen came up and said that our solo was over—three days. I had planned much more communion with my Father. I felt like I still had tons to accomplish. I packed up, and we all met on the road. I was kind of disappointed. I think I could have used two or three more days alone with my Father. Everyone's experience seemed so different from mine. They really hated it and could not wait to leave. I really was just getting into it. I was not quite as hungry either as they expressed they were.

When we got back to the clearing, Karen and Gil had chicken noodle soup, oranges, and tea for us. We were to get with another person—someone we hadn't slept near, camped near, or gotten to know well. Stence and I got together. We were to feed one another. Stence didn't want to do it. She was pretty closed, and I knew we weren't being very honest with each other. She just refused to do it, and said she wasn't hungry. I knew she must have at least been hungry enough for an orange. She didn't want to open herself up to me, so she didn't feed me either. We fed each other soup and tea. Really, I just tipped the cup until she signaled okay. I think it could have been a much better experience. I felt full, but really my stomach was just expanded.

We hiked about a mile and one-half uphill. It was very difficult after not doing physical activity for a couple of days without food. I feel good, but it sure was a rough climb uphill. It is really hot. We had to pose for a picture. I think that is the most stressful. We got to the picnic area. Awaiting us, believe it or not, were two big watermelons. We were in our glory. I washed my hair, my arms, and my underarms. It was so nice. I smell clean, and my hair is clean. Then the finale—I can't believe it! They brought out hot dogs, hamburgers, potato chips, bread, pickles, ketchup, potatoes, hot chocolate, and vegetables. Wow! We are all eating like kings and queens. I must eat slowly so it doesn't come back up.   Lorraine, Jolene, Martha, and I are attempting to get our certification for First Aid in two days. We are devouring this food. I had two hot dogs, a hamburger, pickles, potato chips, hot chocolate (I mean cold chocolate), and half of another hot dog. I think I'm stuffed.

We had a time of sharing. Well, my second pen ran out. We shared a lot about how the Lord really worked in our lives as well as how much we learned about one another and ourselves. It was a very good time speaking of the Lord's goodness and grace. He has given to us so abundantly, and we take so much for granted in our daily lives.

We talked about the Lord's protection. There is so much that can happen to us. There are many opportunities for us to be injured. In our daily lives pain, death, and disaster surround us. We talked about how easy it will be when we go back home to slip back into our old rut and forget what the Lord has done in our lives. We kind of take our defenses down when we are home and slide back into our old patterns. We really prayed for the continued teaching of what we have learned here to be carried out through the rest of our lives. We want so much to apply what we have learned here to our everyday lives when we get back. We talked about our relationships and communication with others and our families. We determined that no matter what we said if our lives didn't show it, it would be useless. We talked more and more intimately as the night went on. It just showed me the infiniteness of God. Oh, the depth of His love.

Jolene and I talked a lot about school and our feelings. Gil and I talked, which was really an uplifting and encouraging time. He said that I was an intense Christian, and that excited him. Oh, I want so much to become close to Jesus. He has given all things to me. He is the origin and the beginning of all things. We can't muster up our faith for Him, that must come from Him. We are sons of the Living God. Rejoice!

We talked about how frustrated we would become when we went home unable to capture experiences into words. We will be frustrated because we will try to learn all of our lessons at once; they will be only half-learned. We need to take each thing God gives us one step at a time, learn it thoroughly, and do it to the best of our ability. One thing at a time, Susan.

We got treated to marshmallows. Can you believe that? Marshmallows and hot chocolate. Wow! I devoured quite a few. We sang around

the campfire, and I shared a little with Joe. It was
such a good evening.

May 27th

Well, this is it—our last full day. It is a beautiful morning. I awakened with the sun and heard the beauty of the birds. I started reading my First Aid book and writing in my journal.

Oh, it is so good to know and love God. He is <u>so</u> <u>good </u>to me. It is good to be alive and well in Him.

Well, this is it. We are doing a junior marathon – 13 miles uphill. I really learned a lot about myself and about the Lord. We had a breakfast bar and Carnation Instant Breakfast. I learned how the Lord wants me to be me-- running at my own pace and not struggling to be ahead of anyone else.   I can't run the race for anyone else. It was nice to run along in the woods. The rocks were pretty rough, but it was really nice to run by our solo sights. I thought of Romans 12:1, Galatians 2:20; Ephesians 5:20; Matthew 6:33, and II Timothy 2:24.

When I got to Gil, it was an accomplishment running up along the highway straight uphill. I didn't want to stop, but for an instant I thought my second cup of Carnation milk would come up. I stopped for a few minutes and kept going. It was probably the roughest going uphill. When I got to Karen, she passed some water to me. The next three and one-half miles were all uphill.

Lorraine just moved from last to first place. She really amazed me—12 miles without stopping. She did it in one hour and 17 minutes. She doesn't even look like she ran. I'm really growing to love her. She has been "catching the rays." I love to hear her talk. She's so expressive. When I thought I was almost done, there would be another hill, another in the mountain, another slope, or another curve. It really taught me about my relationship with the Lord. How many times I think that I'm there—that I've made it—and I still have miles to go.

Mike has become much more sensitive to people and about relationships. He just really pulled from the back to a minute ahead of Lorraine. I got done in one hour and 33 minutes. I didn't have any physical problems and was glad about that. I felt good when I finished. Ernie was a real encouragement and inspiration to me. Lorraine was too. We had watermelon and went to Hale Lake. It is so warm out, and the sun was very refreshing. Everyone got washed up; it was just a nice, relaxing afternoon in the sun. Oh, thank you Lord.

We got into the bus and rode for five hours to arrive at a National Park along with the rest of the Memorial Day crowd. We are getting ready for tuna and macaroni again. It is the fourth time in two weeks, but it sure will be good. We haven't had anything all day. It was kind of funny today. We pulled into a gas station where a group was giving away free refreshments. We all must have looked starved. We kind of felt grubby. They gave us pop and a doughnut. We just could not believe it.

When we realized that we were done and on our way home, we got pretty excited. Jolene and I talked (rather, I talked) almost the whole way home. We looked at the map at all the places we had been. We were only about an hour from Tennessee. I couldn't believe it. We talked about food, and Si left us to go to Atlanta. I thought about all the things I'm looking forward to—the small things I'm going to appreciate such as eating at a table and off a plate with a knife, fork, and spoon. I can't wait to get back on a regular diet and also a regular time of sleeping and running. I'm looking forward to seeing Joyce and Rhoda and my family. We had tuna and macaroni, corn, potatoes, hot chocolate, and lemonade. I had so much that I feel badly that I ate so much. I've got to learn temperance in all things. The Lord is so good! He gives so abundantly. We are really fortunate. We are keeping it down and are ready to go to sleep.

<u>May 28th</u>

Last night was the most difficult night of the trip or possibly of my life. I itched the whole night and possibly slept about two hours if that. There were a few people who slept. I didn't know whether I had a rash or bugs or what. I almost cried. There was a group alongside of us drinking and smoking dope. They disturbed us all night. Everyone just itched themselves to death! I tried to think of other things, but there were bugs all over me. I put my head under my sleeping bag, and two weeks of filth and body odor suffocated me. Oh, the filth. I wanted to cry.

I can't imagine how Paul rejoiced in all things and how he gave thanks in all things. It was such a horrible night that I prayed for everyone I could think of. I prayed for morning to come. I kept looking at the moon; it seemed morning would never come. Well, it's about 5 a.m. Practically everyone ran out of the tent! We want to go home and soon. We are all dragging, filthy, and eating blueberry pancakes. The pictures are snapping.

About the Author:

Susan Briggs Osborn earned a Bachelor of Arts in Health and Physical Education, did coursework in Sociology and attended Saint Vincent School of Nursing, and took Economics at Moscow University.

Susan taught Social Studies on a Navaho Reservation in New Mexico, teaching in public and private schools for many years, and homeschooled her own children in between. Susan also operated her own landscaping and lawn care business for nearly two decades. She is a respected tennis player and avid golfer and has run a half marathon.

Susan is expanding her repertoire currently as a Library Director. No longer hiding behind books, Susan is working on writing her own! She has been married for more than 30years in a row to the same person! She spends time enjoying her three adult children and their spouses and is soon to be a first time Grandmother!

Made in the USA
Middletown, DE
14 March 2023

26741647R00049